# hope anyway

A 30-Day Devotional for the Restless and Worn-Out

The Anchored Devotional Series
Book One

# emery knox

Copyright © 2025 by RMC Publishers

All rights reserved.

No part of this publication may be reproduced in any form, or by any means, electronic or mechanical, including photocopying, recording, or any information browsing, storage, or retrieval system, without prior permission in writing from the publisher.

Under no circumstance will any blame or legal responsibility be held against the publisher, or author, for any damages, reparation, or monetary loss due to the information contained within this book. Either directly or indirectly. You are responsible for your own choices, actions, and results.

Please note the information contained within this document is for educational and entertainment purposes only. All e!ort has been executed to present accurate, up-to-date, and reliable, complete information. No warranties of any kind are declared or implied. Readers acknowledge that the author is not engaging in the rendering of legal, financial, medical, or professional advice. The content within this book has been derived from various sources. Please consult a licensed professional before attempting any techniques outlined in this book.

www.rmcpublishers.com

# foreward

**Oh, To Keep the Flame of Hope Burning**

*Joshua Rivedal*

I was twenty-six the day I contemplated ending my life. I didn't really want to die — I just didn't know how to live with the emotional pain I was carrying. My life felt like it had unraveled. My father had died by suicide. My relationship ended. I felt like a failure in a career I once loved. I kept it all inside — and the silence nearly killed me.

My grandfather also died by suicide. Neither he nor my dad spoke up in time, but deep down I knew I had to. I stepped back from the ledge, picked up the phone, and called my mom. That call — and the brave acts that followed — changed everything. I reached out to friends. Saw a counselor. Journaled. Told the truth. Over the past fifteen years, I've built a life filled with meaning, healing, and the stories of others who've done the same.

One thing I've learned: hope doesn't always arrive with a bang. Sometimes it's the quietest thing in the room — a breath you didn't think you could take, a text you send instead of disappearing, a line in a book that makes you feel less alone. Hope is gritty and stubborn. It's the refusal to believe your worst day is the end of your story.

# foreward

That's what this devotional offers. It doesn't try to wrap up your pain with a shiny bow. It sits with you in the dark. It helps you hold space for exhaustion, confusion, anger, loneliness — and gently reminds you that you still matter.

This book doesn't ask you to fake your way through faith or feelings. It invites you in. It holds space. It gives you tools to cling to hope when everything feels hard. Each day's reflection feels like a conversation, not a lecture.

When I was in the worst of it, I didn't know what I needed. But looking back, I needed something like this — something that could meet me in the mess, that honored my pain and my resilience. That let me move at my own pace, with grace and without pressure.

Here, you can cry on page one. You can show up angry on page ten. You can skip a day and return later. There's no shame in that. *Hope Anyway* — like you — is here for the long haul, the slow climb, the quiet victories.

When I founded The i'Mpossible Project, I did it with the belief that stories save lives. This book continues in that tradition — rooted in vulnerability, honesty, and the deep belief that no matter how messy things feel, your story isn't over.

There is no deadline for healing. No finish line for being "okay." But there is help. There is light. And there are authors — like the one behind this book — who create space so you know: you are not alone.

So take a breath. Open the book. And let quiet, steady, unassuming hope meet you right here.

You're not too far gone. You're not broken beyond repair.

You're still in the story. And there's much more ahead.

— *Joshua Rivedal*

Author, Speaker, Mental Health Advocate

Founder of The i'Mpossible Project

joshuarivedal.com | iampossibleproject.com

# contents

| | |
|---|---:|
| Introduction | vii |
| Day 1: What Is Hope, Really? | 1 |
| Day 2: When You're Not Okay | 5 |
| Day 3: Hope Doesn't Mean You're Not Struggling | 9 |
| Day 4: You Don't Have to Have It All Figured Out | 13 |
| Day 5: When You Feel Like Giving Up | 17 |
| Day 6: When You Feel Invisible | 21 |
| Day 7: You're Allowed to Rest | 25 |
| Day 8: When the Answer Is "Not Yet" | 29 |
| Day 9: Hope Doesn't Mean You're Always Happy | 33 |
| Day 10: You Are Not Too Much | 37 |
| Day 11: When God Feels Silent | 41 |
| Day 12: Don't Rush the Bloom | 45 |
| Day 13: Embracing Uncertainty | 49 |
| Day 14: Your Pace, Not Theirs | 53 |
| Day 15: God Doesn't Waste Anything | 57 |
| Day 16: You Are Not Your Mistakes | 61 |
| Day 17: It's Okay to Change Your Mind | 65 |
| Day 18: Finding Strength in Weakness | 69 |
| Day 19: Chosen on Purpose | 73 |
| Day 20: Your Scars Tell a Story | 77 |
| Day 21: The Power of Small Beginnings | 81 |
| Day 22: Finding Strength in Vulnerability | 85 |
| Day 23: When You Feel Behind in Life | 89 |
| Day 24: When the Future Feels Scary | 93 |
| Day 25: Hope That Grows in the Waiting | 97 |
| Day 26: Made for More | 101 |
| Day 27: Hope That Holds On | 105 |
| Day 28: Hope That Restores | 109 |

Day 29: Hope That Strengthens — 113
Day 30: Anchored in Hope Forever — 117

Conclusion: Stay Anchored — 121
One Last Thing… — 123

# introduction

Hey there —

Let's be real. Life can feel like chaos sometimes. You might be holding a thousand tabs open in your mind, trying to figure out who you are, what you believe, who to trust, and whether any of this actually matters. If that sounds familiar, you're not alone. That restlessness you feel? That ache for something more solid to hold onto? That's exactly what this book is about.

This isn't your typical devotional. You won't find perfect prayers or "just have faith" answers here. You will find space — to breathe, reflect, ask hard questions, and find steady ground when the world around you feels unstable.

We're not chasing shallow hope here. We're anchoring to something deeper.

Because hope isn't just a cute idea or a trending hashtag, it's gritty. It's quiet. Sometimes, it's barely a whisper. It shows up on the days you're spiraling, the nights you cry yourself to sleep, the mornings you can barely get out of bed. And even then, it holds on.

You don't need to fake being okay to be here. If you've ever felt ghosted by God, exhausted by the news cycle, overwhelmed by your own mind, or like you're too far gone to be worthy of peace, this book is for you.

## Introduction

Gen Z is walking through fire: climate anxiety, identity struggles, student debt, political chaos, constant comparison, deconstruction, grief, burnout, and uncertainty about what's next. And yet — you're still here. Still showing up. Still hoping for something better. That's powerful. That's *hope in action*.

So here's what to expect: This is a 30-day devotional designed to meet you where you are; with real talk, real Scripture, and real reminders that your faith doesn't have to be polished to be powerful.

Every day includes:

- A verse of Scripture — not religious fluff, but something tangible to hold onto

- A reflection — honest, conversational, and relevant

- 3 journaling questions — because your voice matters, too

- A one-line affirmation or breath prayer — something grounding to carry with you

- A song — because sometimes music says what words can't

- A creative anchor — an image, metaphor, or quote that makes it all stick

- A simple practice — a way to turn hope into action, even in 60 seconds

You don't have to read this perfectly. If you miss a day, come back when you're ready. If you need to cry, let yourself. If you doubt, you're not disqualified. If you feel seen here, then we're doing something right.

Bring your messy heart. Your open mind. Your tired soul.

You're welcome here.

Let's chase raw, honest, resilient hope, together.

You in?

# day 1: what is hope, really?

**Scripture**

*"Let us hold unswervingly to the hope we profess, for He who promised is faithful."* — Hebrews 10:23 (NIV)

**Reflection**

Hope gets tossed around like glitter—cute, but kind of messy. We say things like "I hope you're okay" or "I hope things get better," but when life hits hard, those phrases can feel empty. So what is hope, really?

Hope is not just positive thinking. It's not crossing your fingers and pretending everything's fine. Real hope is gritty. It's stubborn. It's what gets you out of bed when your chest feels heavy. It's choosing to believe that your story isn't finished, even when the page you're on feels blank.

You've probably been let down by hope before. Maybe you wanted something with your whole heart—healing, love, direction—and it didn't happen. That hurts. It makes you wonder if hope is just a setup for disappointment. But here's the thing: Biblical hope is not about outcomes. It's about anchoring yourself to something steady —a God who doesn't flake, fade, or ghost you when you need Him most.

Hope says, "Yeah, things are hard. But I'm still here." It's that flicker of strength when everything in you wants to quit. Even if you can't see the light yet, hope holds the flashlight.

Hope can look like resilience. Like texting someone when you'd rather disappear. Like putting your phone down and showing up to your real life. Like saying a prayer, even if you're not sure God is listening. Like trying again when you failed yesterday.

Hope isn't always loud. Most of the time, it's quiet and steady. It whispers, "Keep going." It doesn't erase the pain, but it refuses to let the pain have the final word. You don't have to be cheerful to be hopeful. You just have to stay in the story.

Today, hope might look like brushing your teeth, answering that message, or simply breathing and saying, "I'm not giving up." That's enough. That's brave. That's hope.

**Journaling Questions**

- What comes to mind when you hear the word hope?

- Have you ever felt let down by hope? What did that feel like, and what came next?

- What would it look like to have real hope today, even if things don't change right away?

**Real Talk Quote**

Hope isn't hype—it's the fight to believe your story's not over.

**Breath Prayer**

*Inhale*: I'm held.

*Exhale*: I'm not giving up.

## Hope Anyway

**Need a soundtrack for today's reflection?**

Scan to listen to: *"Rescue" by Lauren Daigle.*

**Creative Anchor**

*It doesn't light the whole room—just enough for the next step.*

**Try This**

Text someone: "Hey, I'm thinking of you today. No pressure to respond." Hope multiplies when shared.

# day 2: when you're not okay

**Scripture**

"The Lord is close to the brokenhearted and saves those who are crushed in spirit." — Psalm 34:18 (NIV)

**Reflection**

Let's not pretend—some days are just plain hard. There are mornings when you wake up already tired, afternoons when you feel invisible, and nights when your heart aches for no apparent reason. Whether it's grief, anxiety, burnout, depression, or just a quiet sadness that won't leave, *not being okay* is real and it's more common than we talk about.

There's this unspoken pressure to "be fine" all the time, especially if you're someone of faith. Like somehow loving God should mean you're always happy or grateful or smiling. But that's not real life. Even Jesus wept. Even the strongest prophets in the Bible broke down. Feeling crushed doesn't make you weak, it makes you human.

What's wild is that Psalm 34:18 doesn't say God shows up *after* you've pulled yourself together. It says He's **close** when you're shattered. Not distant. Not silent. Not waiting for you to be stronger. Close. Right in it with you. In your mess. In your sobs. In your numbness. In your doubt.

You don't have to fake it with God. You don't have to pretend everything's fine when it's not. He's not afraid of your sadness, your anxiety, your anger, or your silence. In fact, those raw places might just be the most sacred.

Being broken isn't the end of your story. It might be the place where healing begins—not because you fixed yourself, but because you let yourself *be seen*. God doesn't need you to perform. He just wants you to come as you are, even if "you" today is curled up under a blanket and barely holding it together.

**Journaling Questions**

- What does "not okay" look like for you right now, emotionally, mentally, or spiritually?
- What has helped you feel less alone when you've been struggling in the past?
- What would believing God is closest to you in your most challenging moments mean?

**Real Talk Quote**

God doesn't wait for the edited version of you. He loves you right in the mess.

**Breath Prayer**

*Inhale*: I am not alone.

*Exhale*: I am still held.

## Hope Anyway

**Need a soundtrack for today's reflection?**

Scan to listen to: *"Rise Up" by Andra Day.*

**Creative Anchor**

*Broken crayons still color — Beauty doesn't require perfection.*

**Try This**

Stand in front of a mirror and say (even quietly), "I don't have to be okay to be loved today."

# day 3: hope doesn't mean you're not struggling

### Scripture

"We are hard pressed on every side, but not crushed; perplexed, but not in despair... struck down, but not destroyed." — 2 Corinthians 4:8–9 (NIV)

### Reflection

You've probably been there—smiling in front of people, falling apart when you're alone. Maybe you've shown up to school, work, or even church with your best face on, while inside you feel like you're unraveling. Let's be clear: struggling doesn't mean you're failing. It means you're human.

There's this myth in some faith spaces that having hope means always being upbeat, always grateful, always strong. But Paul, the guy who wrote most of the New Testament literally said he was pressed, confused, and struck down. And still, he wasn't destroyed. That's what real hope looks like. Not perfection. Not emotional control. Just showing up when everything in you wants to quit.

Hope doesn't cancel out struggle. It holds you through it. It's not a bright neon sign screaming "everything's fine." It's more like a flickering candle you protect with your hands when the wind is howling. It doesn't always look powerful. But it is.

There's also something powerful in admitting you're struggling while still choosing to hope. That's not weakness. That's resilience. It's being honest about your pain and still choosing to believe healing is possible. It's letting yourself feel the weight of life without letting it define you.

So if you're struggling today—emotionally, mentally, spiritually—you're not disqualified from hope. You don't have to fake joy to have faith. You can be exhausted and still trust. You can cry and still belong. You can struggle and still grow. You're not broken. You're becoming.

### Journaling Questions

• What's one area of your life where you feel like you're silently struggling right now?

• How do you usually respond to your own pain—with kindness or criticism?

• What might giving yourself grace in the middle of this struggle look like?

### Real Talk Quote

Struggling doesn't mean you're failing, you're still fighting.

### Breath Prayer

*Inhale*: I am not broken.

*Exhale*: I am becoming.

## Hope Anyway

**Need a soundtrack for today's reflection?**

Scan to listen to: *"Beautiful Things" by Gungor.*

**Creative Anchor**

*The cracks don't ruin the story. They're part of the beauty.*

**Try This**

Write one sentence of encouragement you'd say to a friend. Now say it to yourself.

# day 4: you don't have to have it all figured out

**Scripture**

"Trust in the Lord with all your heart and lean not on your own understanding." — Proverbs 3:5 (NIV)

**Reflection**

Here's the truth no one tells you in school: you can't Google your way into peace. You can research, plan, map, and micromanage every area of your life, but some answers only show up after you let go of control.

Letting go doesn't mean giving up. It means loosening your grip. It means choosing to trust even when the outcome is unclear. Faith doesn't always come with bright signs and roadmaps. Sometimes it looks like walking into the unknown with shaky knees and an open heart.

Gen Z gets told you need a plan. Build your brand. Know your niche. Pick a path—before you've even figured out who you are. But here's a radical truth: you are allowed to not have it all figured out. You are allowed to ask questions. To take detours. To pause and wonder. You don't have to force clarity. Sometimes, faith grows in the fog.

God isn't waiting for the "put-together" version of you. He's not watching from a distance until you figure out your purpose or master your mindset. He's walking with you now, in the questions, in the silence, in the slow unfolding.

You don't have to see ten steps ahead. You just have to take the next one. And even if you're unsure where that step leads, He's still guiding. That's what trust is—not knowing, but moving anyway.

**Journaling Questions**

- What's one area of your life where you feel pressure to "figure it all out"?
- What would it look like to release that pressure, just a little?
- When have you experienced peace, even without having all the answers?

**Real Talk Quote**

You don't need all the answers to move forward. Trust grows one step at a time.

**Breath Prayer**

*Inhale*: I don't need to know it all.

*Exhale*: I trust what I can't yet see.

## Hope Anyway

**Need a soundtrack for today's reflection?**

Scan to listen to: *"Take Courage" by Kristene DiMarco*.

**Creative Anchor**

"You don't have to see the whole staircase, just take the first step."
— Martin Luther King Jr.

Let this quote live on your mirror, your lock screen, or in your journal today.

**Try This**

Write down one thing you don't know yet—and next to it, write one thing you do know for sure.

# day 5: when you feel like giving up

**Scripture**

"Let us not grow weary in doing good, for at the proper time we will reap a harvest if we do not give up." — Galatians 6:9 (NIV)

**Reflection**

There are days when getting out of bed feels like a win. When you stare at the ceiling wondering how you'll get through the next hour, much less the rest of the week. Maybe you've been trying—really trying—to stay hopeful, to keep showing up, to do the right thing. And still, it feels like nothing's changing. Like your prayers are hitting the ceiling. Like you're fighting a battle no one else sees.

It's okay to admit that you're tired. Tired of trying. Tired of pushing. Tired of giving your best and watching it fall flat. You're not alone in that. Everyone, even the most faithful hits moments where they want to quit. The moments when it feels like too much, and you don't feel strong or spiritual or motivated. Just empty.

But here's the thing: hope doesn't always look powerful. Sometimes it's quiet. Sometimes it's ugly crying in your car. Sometimes it's dragging yourself to class or work or therapy when you'd rather hide. Hope is staying. Hope is breathing. Hope is deciding that today is not the end.

God doesn't expect you to be perfect. He sees the effort that no one else does. The kindness you offer when your own heart feels hollow. The prayer you mumble when you're not even sure you believe it. The resilience it takes to simply try again. And He honors it.

Galatians 6:9 promises that a harvest is coming, *if we don't give up*. It doesn't say "if you do it perfectly," or "if you never doubt." Just *don't give up*. Keep planting those quiet seeds. Keep taking small steps. You don't have to carry the whole story today. Just turn the page.

**Journaling Questions**

- What's one area of your life where you've felt like giving up lately?
- What would it look like to take just one small step forward today?
- Who or what helps you keep going when you feel empty?

**Real Talk Quote**

Hope doesn't always feel strong. Sometimes it's just staying in the story.

**Breath Prayer**

*Inhale*: My small steps matter.

*Exhale*: I'm still in this.

## Hope Anyway

**Need a soundtrack for today's reflection?**

Scan to listen to: *"Nothing Else" by Forrest Frank.*

**Creative Anchor**

*You don't always see growth happening, but that doesn't mean it isn't.*

**Try This**

Choose one tiny act today—brushing your teeth, texting someone back, going for a walk. And call it victory.

# day 6: when you feel invisible

**Scripture**

"You have searched me, Lord, and you know me… You are familiar with all my ways." — Psalm 139:1, 3b (NIV)

**Reflection**

Have you ever felt like you could disappear and no one would notice? Like you're surrounded by people but still feel unseen? Gen Z is more digitally connected than any previous generation, yet loneliness and invisibility still linger in many hearts.

There's something quietly painful about not feeling known. We're wired for connection — to be understood, chosen, seen. But when likes don't equal love and messages stay unread, it's easy to start believing the lie that you don't matter. That you could vanish, and no one would blink.

But here's what's true: God did before anyone else saw you. Before you had a username, He knew your name. God sees you even when your story feels too messy to share or your presence feels like background noise. Not in a vague, faraway sense — but with attention, with intention, with love.

Psalm 139 isn't just poetry. It's a promise. You are fully known. Every anxious thought. Every unspoken dream. Every habit, fear, and hidden hope. God isn't guessing about who you are. He knows. And still, He stays.

You are not invisible to the One who shaped you. You are not overlooked by the Creator who knit you together. And the more you root your identity in *that*, the less power the silence of others holds over you.

Hope begins when we stop chasing visibility and start believing we're already seen.

### Journaling Questions

- When was a time you felt overlooked or invisible? What made you feel that way?
- How do you usually try to feel "seen" and does it actually help?
- What would change if you truly believed God sees and values you right now?

### Real Talk Quote

God doesn't just tolerate you. He sees you, knows you, and chooses you.

### Breath Prayer

*Inhale*: I am not invisible.

*Exhale*: I am fully known.

### Need a soundtrack for today's reflection?

Scan to listen to: *"Known" by Tauren Wells.*

# Hope Anyway

**Creative Anchor**

Short Story: *The Girl at the Coffee Shop*

She sat at the corner table every Thursday. Same time. Same drink — an oat milk latte with cinnamon. Headphones on, eyes down. People came and went, but she was always there — like background music.

One day, the barista, new to the job, paused while cleaning. "Hey," he said gently, "you always sit here, right? You like the sun coming through the window?"

She looked up, surprised. "Yeah… I guess I do."

He smiled. "I saved this spot for you today. Thought you might like that."

Her throat tightened. No one had noticed her habits before. She wasn't just a body in the room. She was seen.

Later, she'd think about how something so small, someone remembering where she liked to sit could make her feel so human again.

**Try This**

Look someone in the eye today — really see them — and say their name. Let them know they matter.

# day 7: you're allowed to rest

**Scripture**

"Come to me, all you who are weary and burdened, and I will give you rest." — Matthew 11:28 (NIV)

**Reflection**

In a world that constantly tells you to hustle, grind, level up, and "stay productive," rest can feel like rebellion. But it's also sacred. You weren't made to run on empty. You were made to breathe — pause, step away, and let your soul catch up with your schedule.

Maybe you've been feeling guilty for needing a break, like resting means slacking. Like, slowing down means falling behind. But Jesus doesn't call the impressive. He calls the tired. The burned out. The ones whose hearts are heavy and whose minds won't stop racing.

Rest isn't weakness. It's an act of trust. Trust that the world won't fall apart if you take a breath. Trust that your value isn't in how much you produce or perform. Trust that God is still moving even when you're not.

And let's be honest — some days, rest feels harder than work. It can be uncomfortable to stop, get quiet, and face the feelings underneath all the noise. But rest is more than sleep. It's letting yourself be. Unrushed. Undistracted. Unapologetic.

So, if your soul feels louder than your to-do list today, pay attention. If your body feels heavy, listen. You are not lazy, you are not behind, and you are allowed to rest.

**Journaling Questions**

- How do you usually feel about rest — guilty, peaceful, anxious?
- What are some signs your body or soul gives you when you're running low?
- What would rest look like for you today, even just 10 minutes?

**Real Talk Quote**

Rest isn't a reward for doing enough. It's part of being human.

**Breath Prayer**

*Inhale*: I am allowed to slow down.

*Exhale*: I don't have to earn rest.

## Hope Anyway

**Need a soundtrack for today's reflection?**

Scan here to listen to: *"Breathin" by Ariana Grande.*

**Creative Anchor**

Breathwork Prompt:

Try the 4-7-8 breathing pattern. Inhale through your nose for 4 seconds. Hold for 7 seconds. Exhale through your mouth for 8 seconds. Repeat four times. Let your body send the signal: it's safe to rest.

**Try This**

Block off ten minutes today. No phone, no pressure. Just sit, stretch, nap, or breathe — without guilt.

# day 8: when the answer is "not yet"

**Scripture**

"But if we hope for what we do not yet have, we wait for it patiently." — Romans 8:25 (NIV)

**Reflection**

Waiting is hard, especially when you're doing everything "right" and still, nothing. No answer. No change. No breakthrough. Just silence and the ache of *not yet*. That in-between place can feel like a spiritual desert, where hope dries up and you wonder if God forgot you there.

But here's the sacred truth: not all waiting is wasted. Sometimes, what's happening during the pause is as important as what you're waiting for. It might not be about the outcome at all. It might be about who you're becoming while you wait.

We often think of patience as passive. But real patience is active. It's choosing to keep showing up, trusting without a timeline, holding space for something unseen, and still believing it's possible. In waiting, we develop more than endurance—we grow perspective, clarity, and sometimes even peace.

God's timeline rarely syncs with ours. That's frustrating, yes. But it's also freeing. Because if God isn't rushed, we don't have to be either. That "pause" you're living through might be protecting you, preparing you, even healing something you didn't know was broken.

You don't have to pretend the waiting feels good. You don't have to enjoy it. But you can honor it. You can trust that the slow, quiet growth inside you is doing holy work. Something rooted. Something lasting.

You're not being punished. You're being shaped.

**Journaling Questions**
- What are you currently waiting for that feels hard or uncertain?
- How have you grown through past seasons of waiting?
- What would it look like to practice patience without letting go of hope?

**Real Talk Quote**

Waiting isn't wasted when it grows something deep in you.

**Breath Prayer**

*Inhale*: I can wait with hope.

*Exhale*: This season has a purpose.

## Hope Anyway

**Need a soundtrack for today's reflection?**

Scan to listen to: *"Seasons" by Hillsong Worship.*

**Creative Anchor**

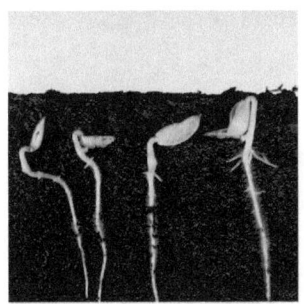

*Just because you don't see it yet doesn't mean it's not becoming something beautiful.*

**Try This**

Write one sentence about what you're waiting for—and next to it, write: "God is not done."

# day 9: hope doesn't mean you're always happy

**Scripture**

"The Lord is close to the brokenhearted and saves those who are crushed in spirit." — Psalm 34:18 (NIV)

**Reflection**

Let's get this straight: hope doesn't mean you're walking around with a permanent smile, pretending everything's fine when it's not. That's performance, not peace. Real hope isn't about fake joy — it's about making space for pain and believing that pain won't have the final word.

You can be full of hope and still cry your eyes out. You can trust God even if you still have doubts. You can be healing and still feel like you're breaking on some days. That tension? It's human. And God isn't scared of it. Not your sadness. Not your silence. Not your spirals. He doesn't withdraw when you break down — He draws closer.

Psalm 34:18 says God is near the brokenhearted, not the cheerful, polished, or optimistic, but near the broken. That means hope is not about pretending you're okay. It's about showing up honestly. It's brushing your teeth when you'd rather stay in bed. It's replying to one message. It's breathing in and saying, "I'm still here." That counts. It all counts.

Hope isn't a performance. It's presence. It's the small decision to keep living, even with a heavy heart. So if you're not okay today, that's okay. You're allowed to feel what you feel. You're allowed to grieve and still believe. You don't have to wear hope on your face for it to be in your spirit.

Let today be honest. Let it be quiet, if that's what you need. Because hope lives in truth, not in hype. And even in heartbreak, you are not alone.

**Journaling Questions**

- When have you felt you had to "fake being okay" for others? Why?
- How does it feel to know that God is near when your heart is breaking?
- What's one small act of hope you can choose today, even if it doesn't feel like much?

**Real Talk Quote**

You can hurt and hope at the same time.

**Breath Prayer**

*Inhale*: My pain is real.

*Exhale*: So is my hope.

## Hope Anyway

**Need a soundtrack for today's reflection?**

Listen to: *"Maybe It's OK" by We Are Messengers.*

**Creative Anchor**

Visual Journal Prompt: Draw or describe what hope would look like if it were a person walking beside you on your worst day. Would they speak? Would they hold your hand? What would their presence feel like?

**Try This**

Choose one small act that brings comfort like lighting a candle, journaling, making your bed, and call it hope.

# day 10: you are not too much

**Scripture**

"I praise you because I am fearfully and wonderfully made; your works are wonderful, I know that full well." — Psalm 139:14 (NIV)

**Reflection**

Have you ever been told, directly or indirectly that you're too intense, too emotional, too opinionated, too much? Maybe someone rolled their eyes when you got excited. Perhaps they told you to calm down, quiet down, or shrink a little. And maybe, over time, you started believing them.

You started editing your voice. Dimming your light. Softening your joy. You began to wonder if being fully yourself was a problem to fix.

But here's the truth: God didn't make a mistake with you. You weren't made to be less. You were never meant to be small.

You were made on purpose, with complexity, passion, fire, sensitivity, intellect, and soul. That's not an accident. That's intentional. The world might not always know what to do with people who feel deeply, think critically, or speak boldly, but God does. He knit you together, and He called you extraordinary. Not after you toned it down. Not after you got quieter. As you are.

Hope begins to grow when you stop apologizing for being whole. When you stop editing yourself to fit into spaces you were never meant to shrink into. The right people, the ones God places in your life won't be intimidated by your light. They'll celebrate it. They'll see your "too much" as the strength it really is.

You don't have to water yourself down to be loved. You don't have to over-explain your heart to be understood. You are allowed to take up space. You are not too much — you are a wonder.

**Journaling Questions**

• Have you ever felt you had to tone yourself down to be accepted? What did that feel like?

• What are some qualities in yourself you once saw as "too much" that might actually be strengths?

• How can you begin to embrace your full self without apology?

**Real Talk Quote**

The people meant to walk with you won't ask you to shrink.

**Breath Prayer**

*Inhale*: I am not too much.

*Exhale*: I am wonderfully made.

Hope Anyway

**Need a soundtrack for today's reflection?**

Listen to: *"You Say" by Lauren Daigle.*

**Creative Anchor**

Quote: "You are not too much. You have never been too much. You are exactly enough." — Brianna Wiest, *The Mountain Is You.*

**Try This**

Write down three things someone once told you were "too much" — then reframe each as a strength.

# day 11: when god feels silent

**Scripture**

"How long, O Lord? Will you forget me forever? How long will you hide your face from me?" — Psalm 13:1 (NIV)

**Reflection**

There's a particular ache in silence, especially when you're praying, reaching, begging for something... and all you get back is stillness. No neon sign. No whisper of comfort. Just quiet. And in that quiet, it's easy to start wondering: *Is God even listening?*

If you've ever asked that question, you're not alone. David did, too. The man called "a man after God's own heart" wrote those exact words in Psalm 13. His raw honesty is what made his relationship with God so deep. Silence doesn't mean absence. But let's be honest — in our humanness, it can feel like abandonment.

The silence of God isn't always punishment. Sometimes, it's space. And space can be sacred. It's where the noise dies down, where we stop performing. Where the masks slip and we sit with what's real. It's uncomfortable. But it's holy.

In silence, we wrestle. We question. We face the hard stuff we've been trying to outrun. And the wild part? God can handle all of it. The anger. The doubt. The "what the heck, God?" kind of prayers.

He doesn't need you to polish your pain. He just wants you to be honest.

Maybe the silence isn't empty. Maybe it's an invitation. Not to do more. Not to fix yourself. But to breathe. To be. To listen in a new way. To trust without clarity. That's hard, but that's where hope grows. Quiet hope. Rooted hope. The kind that holds even when you don't have answers.

### Journaling Questions

- Have you ever felt like God was silent during a hard time? What was that like for you?
- What have you learned about yourself or your faith in quiet seasons?
- How do you want to respond when it feels like you're waiting on God?

### Real Talk Quote

Maybe the silence isn't empty. Perhaps it's sacred space.

### Breath Prayer

*Inhale*: I don't have to hear to be held.

*Exhale*: God is still with me.

## Hope Anyway

**Need a soundtrack for today's reflection?**

Listen to: *"Say Something" by A Great Big World & Christina Aguilera.*

**Creative Anchor**

Instagram Challenge: Create a simple, visual post with the phrase: *"Maybe the silence isn't empty."*

Post it to your story or your feed with the hashtag **#AnchoredHopeDevotional**. If you're feeling brave, share a moment from your own silent season.

**Try This**

Take two minutes of silence today. No music, no prayer words, just presence. Let it be enough.

# day 12: don't rush the bloom

**Scripture**

"To everything there is a season, a time for every purpose under heaven." — Ecclesiastes 3:1 (NKJV)

**Reflection**

Do you ever feel like your life is lagging? Everyone else is glowing up, moving forward, finding love, purpose, direction — and you're still stuck in buffering mode?

It's hard not to compare. Our feeds are full of highlight reels. People are announcing big things like jobs, relationships, and clarity. And meanwhile, you might be staring at your own life, wondering, *Why is everything taking so long for me?*

But here's what we forget: growth doesn't always look like movement. Some of the most critical transformation happens underground — in the quiet, in the stillness, in the slow. Roots go deep, long before anything breaks the surface. Just because you don't see progress doesn't mean you're not growing.

God isn't comparing your timeline to anyone else's. He's not rushing you. He's not disappointed. He's not looking at your pace and saying, "Hurry up." He's saying, *"Be still. I'm working, even now."*

Waiting doesn't mean you're falling behind. It might just mean you're being prepared for something stronger, deeper, and more lasting than you would've chosen. Becoming takes time — real time. And your worth isn't measured by speed or visibility.

So if you're in a season of silence, slowness, or unseen growth, don't rush through it. Honor it. Trust that when your bloom comes, it'll be in its own wild, sacred, exactly-right moment.

### Journaling Questions

- Where in your life do you feel behind or stuck compared to others?
- What unseen growth might be happening in you right now, even if no one else can see it?
- How can you be more patient and kind to yourself while you're waiting to "bloom"?

### Real Talk Quote

Just because it's not blooming yet doesn't mean nothing's happening.

### Breath Prayer

*Inhale*: I trust the process.

*Exhale*: I don't need to rush.

Hope Anyway

**Need a soundtrack for today's reflection?**

Listen to: *"Fight Song" by Rachel Platten.*

**Creative Anchor**

*The moon doesn't rush to be full. It goes through its phases, and each one matters.*

**Try This**

Delete one app or mute one account that constantly makes you feel behind. Protect your pace.

# day 13: embracing uncertainty

**Scripture**

"Trust in the Lord with all your heart and lean not on your own understanding; in all your ways submit to him, and he will make your paths straight." — Proverbs 3:5–6 (NIV)

**Reflection**

Uncertainty might be one of the hardest things to live with, especially in a culture that celebrates clarity, hustle, and five-year plans. You want answers. You want direction. You want to know that all this waiting, wandering, and wondering isn't for nothing.

But life doesn't hand out roadmaps. Most of the time, it feels like walking through fog — you can only see a few steps ahead. And that's terrifying. But maybe it doesn't have to be.

What if trust were the bridge over the unknown? It is not a trust that everything will turn out exactly as you hoped, but a deeper trust. The kind that says, *even if I don't know the plan, I know I'm not walking alone.*

Proverbs 3 doesn't promise clarity. It promises direction, but it's based on trust, not control. Trust is what happens when we stop gripping the wheel and start following a God who sees the whole picture when we only see pieces.

Uncertainty isn't weakness. It's a space where courage is built, faith is stretched, and something new can form. It's not easy, but it can be holy. And sometimes, what feels like losing control is gaining the freedom to explore, discover, and grow.

You don't have to have it all figured out. You just have to keep walking.

**Journaling Questions**

- What uncertainties are you facing right now? How do they make you feel?
- Can you recall a time when not having a plan led to a surprising or positive outcome?
- What would it look like to lean into trust instead of control in this season of your life?

**Real Talk Quote**

Uncertainty isn't a detour — it's part of the path.

**Breath Prayer**

*Inhale*: I release my grip.

*Exhale*: I trust the next step will come.

## Hope Anyway

**Need a soundtrack for today's reflection?**

Listen to: *"Keep Your Head Up" by Andy Grammer.*

**Creative Anchor**

Short Film: *"The Gap" by Ira Glass*

This two-minute animation (search: "The Gap Ira Glass Vimeo") speaks to anyone feeling stuck in the unknown. Originally about creative work, it's deeply relatable to life, reminding us that being unsure doesn't mean you're lost—it means you're growing.

**Try This**

Write down one thing you don't know yet. Then write next to it: "I'm still allowed to move forward."

# day 14: your pace, not theirs

**Scripture**

"Let us run with perseverance the race marked out for us, fixing our eyes on Jesus..." — Hebrews 12:1b–2a (NIV)

**Reflection**

It's hard not to compare. Everyone else seems to be running ahead — getting the job, the relationship, the clarity, the glow-up. Meanwhile, you're here, trying your best and still wondering if you're somehow behind.

But what if you're not behind? What if you're exactly where you need to be?

Life isn't a race with one track and one finish line. It's a journey with turns, pauses, and reroutes. The path marked out for you is different from anyone else's — and that's intentional. God didn't design your story to keep pace with someone else's highlight reel.

When we chase someone else's timeline, we lose sight of our own direction. We exhaust ourselves running a race we were never meant to enter. But God's plans aren't delayed just because someone else seems ahead. What looks like slow progress to you might actually be a sacred season of preparation.

Jesus didn't rush. He wasn't in a hurry to prove His worth. He moved with intention, not urgency. He withdrew when needed. He walked purposefully and trusted that time was not His enemy.

You can too.

Resting doesn't mean quitting. Going slow doesn't mean failing. Growth can be steady. Healing can take time. You don't have to run to go somewhere. Sometimes the bravest thing you can do is walk at your own pace with faith, not comparison.

**Journaling Questions**

• Where in your life are you feeling "behind"? Who or what are you comparing yourself to?

• What would it feel like to release comparison and trust your own timing?

• What's one step, however small, you can take today at your own pace?

**Real Talk Quote**

You're not behind. You're just not running their race.

**Breath Prayer**

*Inhale*: I release comparison.

*Exhale*: I walk with purpose.

## Hope Anyway

**Need a soundtrack for today's reflection?**

Listen to: *"Be OK" by Ingrid Michaelson.*

**Creative Anchor**

Visual Inspiration: TikTok's "slow living" and "soft life" aesthetic

Search "slow living aesthetic" or "soft life TikTok" to see Gen Z creators embracing rest, simplicity, and intentional rhythms. These quiet videos remind us that joy doesn't require speed, and your life doesn't have to move fast to be meaningful.

**Try This**

Unfollow one account that triggers comparison, and replace it with someone who inspires peace, not pressure.

# day 15: god doesn't waste anything

**Scripture**

"And we know that in all things God works for the good of those who love him, who have been called according to his purpose." — Romans 8:28 (NIV)

**Reflection**

What if the thing you regret the most — the heartbreak, the failure, the missed opportunity — is the soil where something beautiful is starting to grow?

It doesn't always feel that way in the moment. Pain can seem random. Waiting can feel like punishment. Mistakes can look like permanent stains. But Romans 8:28 reminds us that God works through *all things* — not just the victories, the parts that make it onto your highlight reel, and the painful, confusing, hidden moments too.

God doesn't waste anything. He doesn't throw away your worst days or forget your most challenging seasons. He gathers them. Redeems them. Repurposes them. Even the parts of your story that feel broken or unfinished are being worked into something purposeful by the One who sees the whole picture.

You may not see it yet, but that chapter you thought was the end could become the beginning of something more honest, more grounded, more real. The wound might become wisdom. The silence might build strength. The delay might prepare you for something greater than you were praying for.

That doesn't mean the pain didn't matter — it means it *does*. And God is determined to use *even that* for your good.

### Journaling Questions

• What's one experience in your past that felt pointless or painful at the time?

• Looking back, can you see anything good that came from it, even in small ways?

• How would it change your mindset if you truly believed God was repurposing your hard seasons?

### Real Talk Quote

Your pain isn't proof that God is gone. It might be the place He's planting something new.

### Breath Prayer

*Inhale*: Nothing is wasted.

*Exhale*: Even this will grow.

## Hope Anyway

**Need a soundtrack for today's reflection?**

Listen to: *"Broken Vessels (Amazing Grace)" by Hillsong Worship.*

**Creative Anchor**

Film Reflection: *Inside Out* (Pixar, 2015)

In *Inside Out*, Riley's emotions — Joy, Sadness, Anger, Disgust, and Fear — all matter. At first, Joy tries to silence Sadness, believing only happiness is valuable. But as the story unfolds, it becomes clear: healing and connection often come through the very moments we want to avoid. Just like in your story, every emotion and experience, even the hard ones, have value.

Prompt: Think about one scene from *Inside Out* that stayed with you. What emotion do you tend to push away? What might it be trying to teach you?

**Try This**

Write a short letter to your past self in one of your lowest moments. Tell them what you've learned — and what God is still doing.

# day 16: you are not your mistakes

**Scripture**

"Therefore, if anyone is in Christ, the new creation has come: The old has gone, the new is here!" — 2 Corinthians 5:17 (NIV)

**Reflection**

We've all made choices we wish we could take back. Words said in anger—decisions made out of fear. We didn't show up how we wanted to or how someone else needed us to.

And those moments? They have a way of sticking. Like invisible name tags: *Unworthy. Failure. Not Enough.* They whisper that you are what you did. That your past is your identity. No matter how much you try, you'll always be that mistake.

But that's not what God says.

2 Corinthians 5:17 doesn't say you're "better." It says you're new. Fully remade. Not edited. Not patched up. *New.* Your worth isn't measured by your worst day or biggest regret. You are not defined by what you did or didn't do, but by what Christ has done for you.

Shame will try to keep you stuck. Grace calls you forward.

And yes, some scars might remain. But even scars can tell stories of healing. Proof that you've grown, that you've survived, that you're still here. Nothing—not even your missteps-wasted in God's hands.

He rewrites what we thought was the end and turns it into something worth sharing.

You are not your past. You are not your shame. You are not your sin. You are His — redeemed, restored, and redefined.

**Journaling Questions**
- What mistake have you been holding onto or letting define you?
- What would change if you believed God makes you new?
- Can you begin to see your story through the lens of grace?

**Real Talk Quote**

You're not your failure. You're God's work-in-progress — and He's not done.

**Breath Prayer**

*Inhale*: I am forgiven.

*Exhale*: I am made new.

# Hope Anyway

**Need a soundtrack for today's reflection?**

Listen to: *"This Is Me" by Keala Settle (from The Greatest Showman).*

**Creative Anchor**

Art Feature: *"Grace Covers It" by Brynne Delerson*

A gentle watercolor of imperfect brushstrokes layered together in harmony. A visual metaphor for what grace does. It doesn't erase the mess. It transforms it into something beautiful.

Prompt: Spend a few minutes reflecting on the image (or imagining it if you can't view it). How might your story look different if you let grace cover it?

**Try This**

Write down a name or label shame has given you — then cross it out and write a new one based on who God says you are.

# day 17: it's okay to change your mind

**Scripture**

"Do not conform to the pattern of this world, but be transformed by the renewing of your mind." — Romans 12:2 (NIV)

**Reflection**

Sometimes we make decisions based on who we used to be. Maybe you said yes to something that no longer fits. Maybe you held a belief about yourself, or about God, that now feels off. Maybe you told the world, *"This is who I am,"* and now you realize you've outgrown that version of yourself.

That's okay. That's growth.

There's this pressure, especially online to stay consistent, to never change your mind, never change direction, never "go back" on what you said or who you were. But Scripture doesn't call us to sameness. It calls us to transformation.

Romans 12 says your mind is supposed to be renewed. That means it changes. That means *you* change. Letting go of an old opinion or identity isn't failure, it's faith in action. It's responding to the Spirit's quiet invitation to become new.

Sometimes, we stay stuck out of pride or fear—fear of looking flaky or being judged. But God doesn't shame you for shifting. He celebrates your willingness to evolve, grow, listen again, and lean in differently.

If you've felt tension lately, like something that used to make sense no longer sits right, pay attention. Maybe God is inviting you to reroute. Maybe there's something new He's trying to teach you. It's okay to pivot. It's OK to change your mind.

**Journaling Questions**

- Is there something you once believed that you no longer do? What changed?
- Where in your life might God be inviting you to reconsider, reroute, or release?
- How can you let go of fear around "looking inconsistent" and trust the process of becoming?

**Real Talk Quote**

Changing your mind isn't a weakness. It's a sign that you're still learning.

**Breath Prayer**

*Inhale*: I am allowed to grow.

*Exhale*: I release what no longer fits.

Hope Anyway

**Need a soundtrack for today's reflection?**

Listen to: *"Let It Go" by James Bay.*

**Creative Anchor**

Short Film: *Self* by Pixar (2024)

This 6-minute animated short tells the story of a wooden doll who longs to fit in and makes a wish that launches her on a journey of transformation. It's a powerful metaphor for identity, conformity, and learning to embrace your true self, not the version others expect.

**Try This**

Write down one idea, identity, or goal you're holding onto out of pressure. Ask: "Is this still true for me?" If not, give yourself permission to release it.

# day 18: finding strength in weakness

### Scripture

"But he said to me, 'My grace is sufficient for you, for my power is made perfect in weakness.' Therefore, I will boast all the more gladly about my weaknesses, so that Christ's power may rest on me." — 2 Corinthians 12:9 (NIV)

### Reflection

We live in a world that praises independence, control, and strength. We're taught to keep it together, fake it 'til we make it, and push through. Admitting weakness? That often feels like failure. Like something to fix or hide.

But God sees weakness differently. In his upside-down kingdom, weakness isn't a flaw — it's a doorway. A place where His power can show up, not despite your struggle, but *through* it.

Paul didn't write these words in triumph. He wrote them in the middle of something hard — something that wouldn't go away. He asked God to take it, and the answer came back: *"My grace is enough. I want to meet you right there — in your not-enough."*

That truth changes everything. When you feel like you can't hold it all, when you're overwhelmed, tired, or quietly breaking, God's not waiting for you to pull it together. He's already there, offering strength that doesn't require you to be strong first.

You don't have to hide your struggle to be loved. You don't have to minimize your pain to belong. Grace doesn't avoid weakness, it meets you in it. And that's where real strength begins.

**Journaling Questions**

- What weakness or struggle have you been reluctant to share with others or God?
- How can you invite God's strength into that area today?
- What would it mean for you to "boast" in your weakness instead of hiding it?

**Real Talk Quote**

You don't have to be strong for God to be strong in you.

**Breath Prayer**

*Inhale*: Your grace is enough.

*Exhale*: Even here, even now.

## Hope Anyway

**Need a soundtrack for today's reflection?**

Listen to: *"Stronger (What Doesn't Kill You)" by Kelly Clarkson.*

**Creative Anchor**

Artwork: *The Starry Night* by Vincent van Gogh

Van Gogh painted this masterpiece during a deeply painful time in his life. And still, it glows. The stars swirl with beauty in the midst of darkness, a reminder that struggle doesn't cancel beauty. In fact, it often deepens it.

Prompt: Look up the painting and reflect what "stars" are present in your own dark night?

**Try This**

Text a trusted friend: "I'm struggling a bit today. Can you pray for me?" Let someone meet you in your weakness.

# day 19: chosen on purpose

**Scripture**

"You did not choose me, but I chose you and appointed you so that you might go and bear fruit—fruit that will last." — John 15:16 (NIV)

**Reflection**

You are not random. You're not invisible. You are not the result of a cosmic accident or a forgotten name on a long list. You were chosen — intentionally, purposefully, and lovingly.

And not by just anyone. God chose you.

Sometimes life makes us feel passed over. Maybe you weren't picked for the team, invited to the group chat, or chosen for the opportunity you hoped for. Rejection can shape how we see ourselves as not enough, not seen, not wanted. But here's the truth that overrides every no: *God chose you.*

Not because of what you've done or earned. Not because you're perfect. But because He sees you. He knows you. He delights in you. And He has something in mind for your life that goes deeper than the surface wins — something lasting.

John 15:16 reminds us that we are chosen to bear *fruit* — to make a difference in this world through how we love, create, encourage, build, and serve. That means you weren't just picked — you were *appointed*. God placed you in this moment in history, in your exact body, with your exact gifts, for a reason.

You didn't stumble into this life. You were sent.

**Journaling Questions**

- How does knowing that God chose you change how you see yourself today?

- What unique gifts or "fruit" do you think you've been created to share with others?

- Where do you feel God nudging you to show up with purpose this week?

**Real Talk Quote**

You weren't just born — you were sent.

**Breath Prayer**

*Inhale*: I am chosen.

*Exhale*: I will live with purpose.

Hope Anyway

**Need a soundtrack for today's reflection?**

Listen to: *"Unwritten" by Natasha Bedingfield.*

**Creative Anchor**

Podcast: *"You're Already Enough" – For The Girl Podcast*

This short episode reminds you that your value isn't something to earn, it's already yours. Centered on identity and calling, it's a gentle but powerful affirmation that you've already been chosen. (Find on Spotify or Apple Podcasts by searching the title.)

**Try This**

Write down three places in your life where you've been questioning your worth — then write next to each: "I was chosen on purpose."

# day 20: your scars tell a story

**Scripture**

"He heals the brokenhearted and binds up their wounds." — Psalm 147:3 (NIV)

**Reflection**

We often treat scars like things to hide — flaws we cover up, memories we'd rather forget. But in God's view, your scars aren't marks of shame. They're signs that healing has already begun. They're proof that what tried to break you didn't win.

Even Jesus, after rising from the grave, kept his scars. He didn't come back flawless. He came back real, whole, wounded, and victorious. Why? Because his scars told a story, not just of pain but of love, not just of death but of resurrection.

Your scars do the same. They tell the truth. About what you've faced. About what you've survived. About what God has brought you through.

Sometimes the world tries to convince us that perfection is the goal. But God isn't looking for polished. He's looking for honest. And your story, with its rough edges and wounded chapters, is exactly the kind of story God uses to bring light to others.

You may carry emotional scars that still feel raw. You may have been through things you rarely speak about. But even those painful places can become powerful when you let God breathe healing into them. Scars don't erase the pain, but show that pain didn't have the last word.

So today, look at your scars with kindness. They are not signs of failure, they are evidence of grace.

**Journaling Questions**

- What scars, physical or emotional, do you carry that still feel raw?
- Can you think of a time when a painful season gave you deeper strength or clarity later on?
- How might your scars help someone else feel less alone?

**Real Talk Quote**

Scars don't mean you're broken. They tell you you've healed.

**Breath Prayer**

*Inhale*: I'm not ashamed of my scars.

*Exhale*: They tell the truth — and God is still writing.

## Hope Anyway

**Need a soundtrack for today's reflection?**

Listen to: *"Scars" by I AM THEY*.

**Creative Anchor**

Instagram Art Series: *"Wounds into Art" by Morgan Harper Nichols*

Morgan's visual poetry and gentle illustrations beautifully affirm healing, pain, and identity. Her art reminds us that what hurts can also become what heals. Search her handle, **@morganharpernichols**

**Try This**

Write a brief "caption" for one of your emotional or physical scars, as if you were posting it to help someone else feel less alone.

# day 21: the power of small beginnings

**Scripture**

"Do not despise these small beginnings, for the Lord rejoices to see the work begin." — Zechariah 4:10 (NLT)

**Reflection**

You might think what you're doing is too small to matter. A quick prayer. A half-formed journal entry. A single kind text. But in God's economy, small isn't insignificant. Zechariah 4:10 tells us that God *rejoices* not when we've finished the work, but when we *begin*.

That's a radically different way of seeing things.

We live in a world obsessed with fast, visible, and measurable results. But most transformation doesn't happen that way. Most healing starts with quiet courage. Most growth begins in hidden places. The work that truly matters often starts small: one "yes," one confession, one moment of showing up when it would've been easier to stay silent.

Maybe you're waiting to feel more ready. More equipped. More "together." But beginnings rarely feel glamorous. They feel uncertain. Risky. Underwhelming. And still they matter.

God sees the seed planted long before the fruit appears. He sees the first step, the wobbly faith, the tiny movement forward, and rejoices. Not because it's perfect, but because it's *real*.

Don't underestimate what's unfolding in this very moment. Even a small beginning can lead to something holy.

**Journaling Questions**

• What's one "small beginning" in your life right now — something that feels minor but matters to you?

• Have you ever looked back and realized a little step led to something bigger than you expected?

• How can you remind yourself that small doesn't mean insignificant?

**Real Talk Quote**

A tiny step in the right direction still moves you forward.

**Breath Prayer**

*Inhale*: I will begin.

*Exhale*: Small is still sacred.

## Hope Anyway

**Need a soundtrack for today's reflection?**

Listen to: *"Lost Cause" by Billie Eilish*.

Though often interpreted as a breakup anthem, the mood of this song evokes the quiet resolve of letting go and moving forward, one step at a time.

**Creative Anchor**

Watch: *"The Butterfly Effect: How Small Actions Change the World" by Andy Andrews* (YouTube). This short, inspiring video unpacks how one choice can ripple into history — a modern take on the idea that our smallest actions may be more powerful than we imagine.

**Try This**

Write down one small thing you're committing to this week; no pressure, just intention. Then underline it and say aloud: "This is enough to start."

# day 22: finding strength in vulnerability

**Scripture**

"Be strong and courageous. Do not be afraid; do not be discouraged, for the Lord your God will be with you wherever you go." — Joshua 1:9 (NIV)

**Reflection**

Vulnerability is often misunderstood. We're told to "stay strong," "keep it together," "fake it 'til you make it." But what if real strength doesn't look like being unshakable? What if it looks like opening your heart, asking for help, admitting you're scared?

Being vulnerable isn't weakness. It's one of the most courageous things you can do. It takes guts to be honest about your fears. To say, *"I'm not okay today."* To reach out when you'd rather retreat. Vulnerability asks you to show up without the guarantee of how you'll be received, and that's bravery.

Joshua 1:9 says to be strong and courageous. But it doesn't mean to be emotionless or self-sufficient. It means stepping forward even when you're trembling. It means letting God's presence strengthen you, not your perfection.

God's idea of courage leaves room for your humanity.

Being vulnerable opens doors to real connection with God, others, and yourself. It breaks the illusion that we have to do life alone and creates space for grace to rush in.

You don't have to pretend. You don't have to fix everything first. When choosing vulnerability, you choose growth, healing, and deeper relationships. You're saying: *"I trust that honesty will carry me further than performance ever could."*

Your realness is not a liability. It's a superpower.

**Journaling Questions**

- When was the last time you allowed yourself to be truly vulnerable? How did it feel?
- What fears hold you back from being open about your struggles?
- How might embracing vulnerability help you build stronger relationships with yourself, others, or God?

**Real Talk Quote**

Being authentic isn't reckless. It's how healing begins.

**Breath Prayer**

*Inhale*: I am safe to be real.

*Exhale*: God meets me in my honesty.

Hope Anyway

**Need a soundtrack for today's reflection?**

Listen to: *"Who Says" by Selena Gomez.*

This gentle, empowering anthem reminds you that your worth isn't up for debate. Vulnerability is part of being beautifully, boldly human.

**Creative Anchor**

Watch: *"The Power of Vulnerability"* — *TED Talk by Brené Brown*

This viral talk dispels the myth that vulnerability is weakness. Brené Brown explains how openness is actually the birthplace of joy, love, and connection.

**Try This**

Reach out to someone you trust and say, "I've been carrying a lot lately, can I share with you?" Then let yourself be heard.

# day 23: when you feel behind in life

**Scripture**

"There is a time for everything, and a season for every activity under the heavens." — Ecclesiastes 3:1 (NIV)

**Reflection**

Everyone seems to be sprinting toward something — a degree, a dream job, a picture-perfect relationship, a platform, a plan. And maybe you feel like you're just trying to breathe. Maybe you're stuck in slow motion while everyone else is speeding ahead. And comparison? It creeps in fast.

*They're already doing X. I haven't even started.*

*They're building a life. I'm still figuring out who I am.*

It's exhausting, and honestly, discouraging. But here's the thing: life is not a race. You're not late. You're not falling behind in some universal timeline. You're just on *your* path.

Ecclesiastes 3:1 reminds us that there is a season for everything. Not everything all at once. Not now-or-never. There is time. And God's timeline is rooted in love, not pressure. Not performance. Not perfection. You don't have to "catch up" to anyone else's pace. Your story unfolds in its own rhythm.

Hope means choosing to believe that this moment — this messy, quiet, uncertain season — still matters. That God is doing something in you, even if it isn't loud or visible. Maybe this is your season of healing. Or becoming. Or listening. Or letting go. And that counts.

You are not behind. You are right where you need to be to become who you're meant to become.

Let go of the myth that there's one perfect timeline. You're not falling behind — you're unfolding.


**Journaling Questions**

- Where in your life do you feel "behind" compared to others?
- What would it feel like to release the pressure to catch up?
- Can you name something meaningful that's growing in you during this season?


**Real Talk Quote**

You're not late. You're living a life that doesn't need to be rushed.


**Breath Prayer**

*Inhale*: I am not behind.

*Exhale*: I am exactly where I need to be.


**Need a soundtrack for today's reflection?**

Listen to: *"Growing Pains" by Alessia Cara.*

This honest anthem captures the struggle of being in progress, not having it all together, and still showing up.

## Hope Anyway

**Creative Anchor**

*Even nature takes its time — and never apologizes for it.*

**Try This**

Write a letter to your future self — not to "fix" anything, but to thank her/him/them for being patient. Then underline one line and say: *"I'm proud of where I am today."*

# day 24: when the future feels scary

**Scripture**

"For I know the plans I have for you," declares the Lord, "plans to prosper you and not to harm you, plans to give you a future and a hope." — Jeremiah 29:11 (NIV)

**Reflection**

The future can feel like one giant question mark. What if things don't work out? What if you choose wrong? What if you waste your time, energy, and one wild and precious life?

Those thoughts can spiral fast. Especially when everyone seems to have a plan or a path, and you're just trying to figure out where to begin.

But this verse from Jeremiah reminds us of something quiet but powerful: God already sees what's ahead. And he's not guessing. His plans for you aren't vague, fragile, or conditional. They are good. And they come with a promise *not to harm you, but to give you a future and a hope.*

Hope doesn't require having it all figured out. It just requires trust in the One who does.

God's plans aren't undone by your detours. They're not dependent on perfect decisions. If you've been paralyzed by fear of messing up the future, breathe. You're not that powerful. You can't ruin what God can redeem. And he's in the business of taking fear and turning it into purpose.

Yes, the future can be overwhelming. But you don't have to live ten steps ahead. You don't have to predict every outcome. You just have to take the next step in faith, trusting that even in the fog, you're not walking alone.

Your job isn't to control the future. It's to trust the One who holds it.

### Journaling Questions

- What part of the future makes you feel most afraid or uncertain?
- How would your mindset shift if you truly believed God had good plans for you?
- What's one small step you can take today, even if you're unsure?

### Real Talk Quote

You don't have to see the whole road to keep moving forward.

### Breath Prayer

*Inhale*: God is already ahead of me.

*Exhale*: I trust what I can't yet see.

### Need a soundtrack for today's reflection?

Listen to: *"Keep Holding On" by Avril Lavigne.*

A soft, empowering anthem for moments when fear rises but you choose to keep walking anyway.

# Hope Anyway

**Creative Anchor**

*You don't have to see the whole road. Just take the next step.*

**Try This**

Write a short prayer or mantra you can come back to when the future feels overwhelming. Start with: *"Even if I don't know what's next, I will..."*

# day 25: hope that grows in the waiting

**Scripture**

"But if we hope for what we do not yet have, we wait for it patiently." — Romans 8:25 (NIV)

**Reflection**

Waiting is hard, especially when you're holding onto hope for something that feels far away—healing, direction, clarity, a door to finally open. It's that in-between space where you're doing your best to trust, but you still wonder, *Is anything actually happening?*

It can feel like standing still while everyone else moves forward. Like you're doing everything "right" — praying, listening, showing up — but nothing seems to shift. And maybe part of you starts to wonder if hope was just a setup for disappointment.

But here's the truth: hope doesn't die in the waiting. It *grows* there.

Quietly. Deeply. Like roots stretching beneath the surface, where no one sees. The waiting isn't empty, it's where God is preparing you. Strengthening you. Shaping you to carry the thing you're praying for. Not just to receive it, but to hold it well.

Romans 8:25 doesn't tell us to wait perfectly. It tells us to wait patiently, the kind that trusts God is still moving, even when we can't trace it. The kind that believes growth can be silent and still sacred.

Waiting isn't punishment. It's preparation.

The waiting room of your life may feel silent, but it's never wasted in God's story. It's the place where your roots go deep, where you learn to release control. Where you begin to believe that delay does not mean denial.

So, if today feels like another quiet day in the middle of not-yet, take heart: God is still working, and your hope is still growing.

**Journaling Questions**
- What are you currently waiting for that feels heavy or slow?
- Can you think of a time when God showed up after a long season of waiting?
- How can you shift your perspective on waiting from frustration to preparation?

**Real Talk Quote**

Waiting doesn't mean nothing's happening. It means something deep is growing.

**Breath Prayer**

*Inhale*: I am being prepared.

*Exhale*: I will trust the quiet.

**Need a soundtrack for today's reflection?**

Listen to: *"Invisible String" by Taylor Swift*.

A soft, poetic track about unseen purpose and quiet timing.

## Hope Anyway

**Creative Anchor**

*Hope doesn't always come loud. Sometimes it rises slowly, but it always rises.*

**Try This**

Write a short letter to your future self, the one who has received what you're waiting for. Let them know it was worth it to wait.

# day 26: made for more

**Scripture**

"For we are God's masterpiece. He has created us anew in Christ Jesus, so we can do the good things he planned for us long ago." — Ephesians 2:10 (NLT)

**Reflection**

Feeling small in a world that constantly asks you to be *more is easy* —more impressive, more productive, more perfect. The pressure to prove yourself can be overwhelming, like you're one step behind or never quite enough.

But Scripture tells a different story. You are not ordinary. You are not accidental. You are not here just to survive the day or chase someone else's version of success.

You are a *masterpiece*.

Let that sink in. Not a project. Not a mess. A masterpiece. Created with care, intention, and infinite worth. The hands of the Creator shaped you, and He doesn't make mistakes.

Even on the days when you feel unsure of yourself. Even when your path looks foggy and the world feels like it's moving on without you, you are still His. And he has *good things* in mind for you. Not someday. *Now.* Right in the middle of your doubts, your waiting, your questions.

Ephesians 2:10 says you were created anew in Christ *to do good things* — things planned long ago. That means your life already has purpose built into it. You don't have to chase it. You just have to *trust* it.

So instead of exhausting yourself trying to measure up, take a breath. Rest in the truth that you were made for more. Not more pressure. More *purpose*. More courage. More love. More joy.

You don't have to prove your worth. You just have to live with it.

**Journaling Questions**

• What does it mean to you to be God's masterpiece?

• How can knowing you have a purpose change the way you face challenges?

• What "good things" might God be inviting you to do, even in small, quiet ways?

**Real Talk Quote**

You don't have to hustle for worth. You already have it.

**Breath Prayer**

*Inhale*: I am created with purpose.

*Exhale*: I was made for more than pressure.

**Need a soundtrack for today's reflection?**

Listen to: *"Bigger Than Me" by Louis Tomlinson.*

This reflective anthem reminds us that we're part of something beyond ourselves — that our lives hold more purpose than we can always see.

# Hope Anyway

**Creative Anchor**

*Even in unexpected places, God's masterpiece blooms — just like you.*

**Try This**

Write "God's masterpiece" somewhere you'll see it today — your mirror, journal, or phone lock screen — as a quiet but bold reminder of who you really are.

# day 27: hope that holds on

**Scripture**

"Be strong and take heart, all you who hope in the Lord." — Psalm 31:24 (NIV)

**Reflection**

Hope isn't always bright and breezy. Sometimes it feels like a flickering candle in the dark or like clutching a single thread in the middle of a storm. There are days when hope doesn't look like confidence. It looks like it's barely hanging on.

But even then, *especially then*, it matters.

Psalm 31:24 doesn't call you to be perfect. It calls you to be *strong* and *take heart*. Why? Because your hope isn't floating, it's *anchored*. It's held by the One who doesn't move, even when everything else around you feels like it's falling apart.

God isn't asking you to carry hope by yourself. He's holding you *while* you hold on. And even when your grip feels weak, His never is.

Hope in the Lord isn't naive optimism. It's not pretending you're okay when you're not. It's the quiet, stubborn belief that God is still with you, still writing your story, still working through your pain, still bringing you toward peace.

And yes, some days will feel heavy. You'll be tired. You'll question. You'll want to quit. But hope isn't the absence of struggle, it's the strength to keep showing up anyway. To say, *"I don't know what's next, but I'm still here. Still holding on."*

That matters more than you know.

You don't have to feel strong to be strong. You just have to keep trusting the One who is.

### Journaling Questions

- When have you felt like giving up, but chose to hold on?
- How can you remind yourself to be strong in times of doubt?
- What small step can you take today to keep hope alive?

### Real Talk Quote

Hope doesn't always shout. Sometimes it just whispers, *"Try again tomorrow."*

### Breath Prayer

*Inhale*: I am held.

*Exhale*: My hope is still alive.

### Need a soundtrack for today's reflection?

Listen to: *"Hold On" by Chord Overstreet.*

This tender song gently reminds us that the hard moments don't last forever and that sometimes, hope is simply the decision to stay one more day.

# Hope Anyway

**Creative Anchor**

*Hope holds on, even when the winds blow hard.*

**Try This**

Text someone you trust: "I'm holding on today, but it's hard." Let someone remind you that you don't have to hold on alone.

# day 28: hope that restores

**Scripture**

"The Lord is close to the brokenhearted and saves those who are crushed in spirit." — Psalm 34:18 (NIV)

**Reflection**

Hope doesn't mean you'll never feel pain. It doesn't mean you'll always feel strong or that the sadness will disappear overnight. It means this: *even in your brokenness, God is near.*

Psalm 34:18 is one of those verses that doesn't just offer comfort, it offers presence. God is *close* to the brokenhearted. Not distant. Not passive. But near. Right there in the middle of your ache, your confusion, your tears. He sees what hurts. And He comes close, not to shame or fix or rush you, but to heal.

When life feels heavy, when you're carrying more than you know how to hold, when your spirit feels crushed by what didn't go right or what you've lost… this is where restoration begins.

Hope isn't always loud. Sometimes it shows up like a whisper: *"You're not alone. This isn't the end. Healing is still possible."*

And restoration? It rarely comes in one dramatic moment. It usually unfolds slowly, like morning light rising over a quiet lake. It's gentle. Patient. Sometimes, so quiet you barely notice it until one day, you realize you're breathing deeper, walking lighter, feeling whole in places you once thought would always be broken.

God doesn't just patch you up and send you on your way. He rebuilds. He makes something *new*. His hope doesn't deny what you've lost, it transforms what's left into something meaningful.

Your brokenness isn't the end of your story. It's the soil where something beautiful can grow.

### Journaling Questions
- What areas of your life feel broken or heavy right now?
- How can you invite God's healing presence into those places?
- In what ways have you experienced restoration in the past?

### Real Talk Quote
You don't have to be whole to be healing — just open.

### Breath Prayer
*Inhale*: God, come close.

*Exhale*: Restore what feels lost in me.

### Need a soundtrack for today's reflection?
Listen to: *"Bright Days" by Blessing Offor.*

A soulful reminder that even in the waiting, brighter days are still ahead.

# Hope Anyway

**Creative Anchor**

*In the quiet, hope whispers the promise of restoration.*

**Try This**

Take a few minutes of stillness today. Put on the song, close your eyes, and imagine God gently restoring the places in you that feel tired, torn, or forgotten.

# day 29: hope that strengthens

**Scripture**

"But those who hope in the Lord will renew their strength. They will soar on wings like eagles; they will run and not grow weary, they will walk and not be faint." — Isaiah 40:31 (NIV)

**Reflection**

Hope doesn't just lift your spirits, it renews your strength. It's not fluffy optimism. It's not denial. Hope is a force — steady and powerful — that shows up when you're tired, worn thin, and unsure how to keep going.

Isaiah 40:31 doesn't say "those who hustle harder" will find strength. It says *those who hope in the Lord*. That kind of hope gives you the stamina to keep walking, the courage to keep showing up, and the grace to rise above what's trying to pull you down.

Some days, hope helps you soar. Other days, it enables you to take one shaky step at a time. Either way, it strengthens you.

When life pushes hard, hope reminds you that you are not alone, and that your story isn't finished. Like an eagle rising above the storm, hope lifts you beyond your limits, not by removing the challenges, but by carrying you through them.

So today, hold onto hope with both hands. Let it remind you of who you are, what you've come through, and how far you can still go.

**Journaling Questions**

- When have you felt renewed by hope during a difficult time?
- What practical ways can you nurture hope daily to strengthen yourself?
- How can you encourage others to find hope and strength in their struggles?

**Real Talk Quote**

Hope is what holds you up when everything else wants to weigh you down.

**Breath Prayer**

*Inhale*: Hope renews me.

*Exhale*: Strength rises in me.

**Need a soundtrack for today's reflection?**

Listen to: *"One Day" by Cochren & Co.*

Hopeful and faith-filled, this anthem points to a day when all things are made right.

# Hope Anyway

**Creative Anchor**

*With hope, I rise above challenges and find the strength to keep going.*

**Try This**

Do something small today that reminds your body or soul what strength feels like — stretch, breathe deeply, or take a walk. Let it be an act of hope.

# day 30: anchored in hope forever

**Scripture**

"May the God of hope fill you with all joy and peace as you trust in him, so that you may overflow with hope by the power of the Holy Spirit." — Romans 15:13 (NIV)

**Reflection**

You've journeyed through 30 days of honest reflection — through the messy middle of doubt, the quiet moments of healing, and the bold decision to hold onto hope anyway.

But this isn't the end. It's the beginning.

Hope isn't a one-time feeling, it's an anchor for your soul. It's what holds you steady when life shakes. What pulls you forward when you feel stuck? What glows quietly in the dark when you can't yet see the light?

Romans 15:13 reminds us that *hope isn't something we create alone.* It overflows from God, the trustworthy source of joy and peace, not because everything is perfect, but because He is present.

You've seen that hope can whisper. It can roar. It can take root in silence and rise up in storms. You've seen that healing is slow but steady. That your story matters. That you are not alone — and never have been.

So wherever you go next, carry this with you:

Hope is your steady. Your strength. Your reminder that light is still ahead.

You are anchored in something that can't be shaken.

**Journaling Questions**

- How has your understanding of hope changed over the past 30 days?
- What habits or practices will you keep to nurture hope in your daily life?
- How can you be a beacon of hope for someone else in your community?

**Real Talk Quote**

Hope doesn't end here. It goes with you — everywhere.

**Breath Prayer**

*Inhale*: I am anchored.

*Exhale*: Hope flows through me.

**Need a soundtrack for today's reflection?**

Listen to: *"Light On" by Maggie Rogers*.

This upbeat, heartfelt song is about shining your light, staying grounded, and embracing growth—even when it's hard. It's a perfect final note to carry forward.

# Hope Anyway

**Creative Anchors**

*Hope is your lighthouse—steadfast, guiding you safely through every storm.*

**Try This**

Write a letter to your future self — a reminder that you've walked through storms before, and you'll walk through whatever comes next. End it with this sentence: *"I am anchored in hope — always."*

# conclusion: stay anchored

Hey there,

You made it.

Thirty days of showing up. Of wrestling with truth, with yourself, with God. Thirty days of asking hard questions, daring to hope again, and letting your guard down, even if only for a moment. That's no small thing. In a world that tells you to numb out or gloss over, you chose presence. That's sacred.

Maybe you started this journey feeling restless. Maybe you were grieving. Searching. Questioning. Or maybe you just wanted something to hold onto in a world that often feels like it's slipping sideways. However you arrived, you're here. And that's what matters.

Hope is not a one-time fix. It's not the kind of thing you "get" and never struggle with again. It's a rhythm. A practice. A quiet yes in the middle of the storm. Sometimes it flickers. Sometimes it glows. And sometimes, it's just barely enough to get out of bed — but even then, it's real.

You might still have questions. You might still be hurting. That's okay. *Hope never required perfection. It only asks that you stay open.* Open to healing. To wonder. To the slow, beautiful work of becoming. It asks that you keep walking, even with shaking knees and blurry vision.

## Conclusion: Stay Anchored

What you've done here matters. Because every time you paused to reflect, breathe, and write something down, you were planting something. And whether you see the fruit of it yet or not, those roots are growing.

So what now?

You keep going. You carry the pieces of this journey with you — a breath prayer when anxiety hits, a verse scribbled on a mirror, a song that holds you when nothing else does. You lean into truth. You reach for community. You let yourself break and rebuild. And you remember: hope isn't just an emotion, it's an anchor. One that holds, even when you don't feel steady.

Maybe you need to reread a few pages. Perhaps you share this book with someone else who's hurting. Maybe you can start a new journal and let your story unfold. Whatever your next step is, take it knowing you are seen, loved, and *not alone.*

Hope is fierce. Hope is messy. Hope is yours.

So here's to the days ahead — to sunrises and setbacks, to new mercies and deep questions. Here's to growing roots in the dark and daring to bloom anyway.

And when the world tries to make you forget who you are, come back here. Read these pages again. Remind yourself: *You are anchored. You are becoming. You are held.*

Keep shining.

Keep breathing.

Keep believing.

With all my heart,

— Emery

# one last thing...

If this devotional helped you hold on to hope,

even just a little, would you consider leaving a quick review?

Your words might be the nudge someone else needs

to take the first step on their own journey.

It doesn't have to be long. Just honest.

Thanks for being here.

Thanks for staying open.

With love,

— **Emery**